BACKWARD SCIENCE

CLIVE GIFFORD

ILLUSTRATED BY ANNE WILSON

QEB

Q Quarto Knows

Quarto is the authority on a wide range of topics.

Quarto educates, entertains and enriches the lives of our readers—enthusiasts and lovers of hands-on living.

www.quartoknows.com

Art Director: Susi Martin
Designer: Kevin Knight
Editor: Harriet Stone
Editorial Director: Laura Knowles
Creative Director: Malena Stojic
Publisher: Maxime Boucknooghe

© 2020 Quarto Publishing plc

This edition first published in 2020 by QEB Publishing,
an imprint of The Quarto Group.
26391 Crown Valley Parkway, Suite 220
Mission Viejo, CA 92691, USA
T: +1 949 380 7510
F: +1 949 380 7575
www.QuartoKnows.com

A CIP record for this book is available from the Library of Congress.

ISBN 978 0 7112 4990 5

Manufactured in Guangzhou, China EB082020

9 8 7 6 5 4 3 2

FSC
www.fsc.org

MIX
Paper from
responsible sources
FSC™ C124385

CONTENTS

INTRODUCTION

Stop! Take a look around. You're surrounded by inventions that make your life safer, easier, more exciting, informing, and entertaining.

Your home is packed with life-enhancing innovations, from central heating and flushing toilets, to TVs with hundreds of channels. Outside, you can travel fast in cars, buses, or trains, while jet airliners roar overhead, transporting people all around the planet. Digital devices such as smartphones and tablets let you communicate with anyone, anywhere in the world, and if you get injured or ill, high-tech hospitals are packed with inventions to make you better.

But things weren't always this way, so how did we get here? This book is your time-traveling guide. It runs backward, starting at the end and ending at the beginning. You will venture further and further into history, to a time before each invention existed.

Get ready, turn the page, and head back in time...

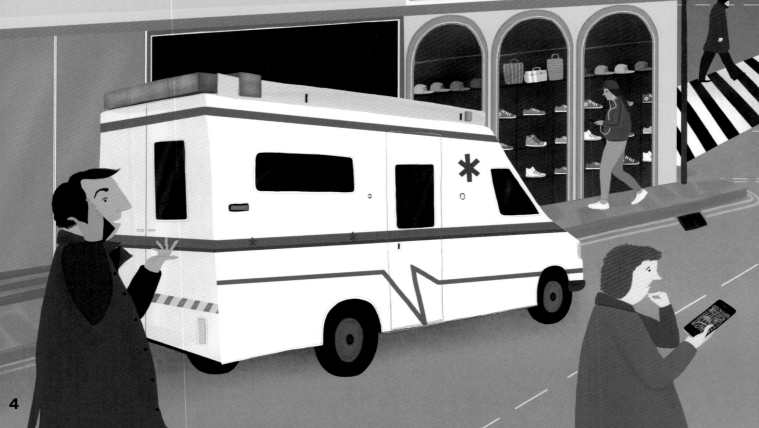

SHOES GALORE

SMARTPHONES AND SATELLITES

Everyday life before smartphones and satellites was so, so different than now. You might write long letters to faraway friends, rather than sending speedy messages via social media. For fun, you might rent a movie from a store, rather than stream it to your smartphone or TV. Without texts and instant messaging, you'd miss out on meeting friends unless you agreed on a particular time and place in advance. Phone calls could be made away from home, but only using a phone booth, and when finding your way in a new place, you'd rely on a printed map or asking strangers for directions.

INVENTION: MOBILE PHONE

The first handheld mobile phones were invented in the 1970s. They converted voice calls into radio waves, which were relayed between radio transmitters. Motorola's DynaTAC 8000X was the first to go on sale in 1983 for $3,995. At 13 inches (33 cm) tall, it weighed ten times as much as a mobile phone today, yet could only make 30 minutes of calls before its battery needed recharging!

SMARTPHONES

Mobile phones got smarter in the 1990s, adding features such as touchscreens, email messaging, and website browsers. Simon, developed by US electronics engineer Frank Canova in 1992, was the first smartphone. Fifteen years later, Apple released its first iPhone, a year before the first Android smartphone. There are now more than 3.1 billion Apple and Android smartphones around the world.

APP ATTACK!

In 2008, both Apple and Android opened smartphone stores where users could download games and programs called apps. Video streaming and social media apps such as Instagram, Twitter, and Facebook give smartphone users fast, easy ways to contact people and share information, photos, and videos instantly.

SPACE SATELLITES

In 1957, the first artificial satellite, a beachball-sized metal sphere called Sputnik, was launched into space and orbited Earth for three months. More than 1,800 satellites now orbit Earth, performing useful tasks such as relaying TV and telephone signals from one part of the planet to another. A large group of satellites work together as the Global Positioning System (GPS) to provide maps and navigation to GPS receivers inside smartphones, smartwatches, or car satellite navigation systems.

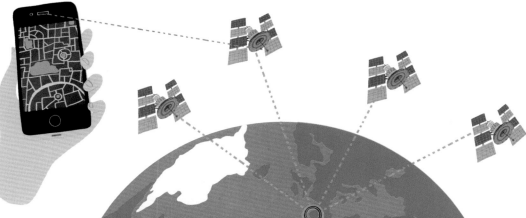

7

DNA PROFILING

Flash! If you were a police officer at a crime scene before DNA profiling, a police photographer would take photos, while you and other officers bagged objects that might be useful to the investigation. You'd dust surfaces and objects for fingerprints to identify who had been at a crime scene earlier, but if the criminal wore gloves or there were many different fingerprints, cracking the case could be difficult.

DISCOVERY: CODE OF LIFE

Information about how a living thing looks and works is stored in the cells as a long strip of deoxyribonucleic acid, better known as DNA. If one of your cell's DNA were unraveled, it would measure around 67 inches (1.7 m) long! The structure of human DNA was first discovered by James Watson and Francis Crick in 1952, along with X-ray photographer Rosalind Franklin.

INVENTION: DNA FINGERPRINTING

While everyone's DNA is alike, there are crucial differences between each person. In 1984, British scientist Alec Jeffreys invented a technique called DNA fingerprinting (later known as DNA profiling). It became possible for a lab to analyze DNA from just a small drop of blood or a few skin cells. Because of unique patterns in the DNA, Jeffreys found it was possible to work out exactly who the DNA came from.

CASE CRACKER

To begin with, DNA profiling was only used to prove whether people were related. In 1987, it was first successfully used in the UK to help solve a murder case, when crime-scene DNA matched a sample taken from a suspect. Samples today are often taken from inside the mouth using a cotton bud swab.

DNA DETECTIVES

Police at a crime scene today are always on the lookout for DNA samples. Even a single hair or fleck of saliva can be crucial. They comb the scene, being careful not to contaminate anything, and may collect many samples to compare to thousands in their computer database, trying to find a match.

9

THE WORLD WIDE WEB

Before the World Wide Web, information was only at your fingertips if you had the right book in your hands! If your parents or home bookshelf couldn't answer your question, it was off to the library. Your search for answers could take time as you combed through lots of books, magazines, or newspapers. Although your family might have an early home computer, there were no websites or search engines. Researchers, journalists, and other information workers often spent days in specialized libraries hunting down key facts.

INVENTOR: TIM BERNERS-LEE (b. 1955)

In 1980, British programmer Tim Berners-Lee wrote ENQUIRE, a program to keep track of people and projects at a science center in Switzerland. Berners-Lee's program used links between pieces of information called hyperlinks. Clicking on a hyperlink sent you to another piece of information. In 1989–90, he developed a global version of ENQUIRE called the World Wide Web. The first website (http://info.cern.ch) was available from August 1991.

WEBSITES

A website is a collection of documents that are stored on a computer, called a web server. Each page of a website (a webpage) has its own unique address called a URL. All webpages are marked up using a special language called HTML, which allows them to be accessed via the Internet by any computer.

INFORMATION BOOM

The World Wide Web began slowly. By June 1993, there were only 130 websites in the world. As more and more people gained Internet access, website numbers soared to 17 million by 1999 and more than 800 million today. Many websites, including newspapers and encyclopedias, contain vast amounts of useful information only previously available on paper. People can now access and share information rapidly from anywhere in the world.

INVENTION: SEARCH ENGINES

As website numbers boomed, it became difficult to find the information you wanted. Search engines are programs that comb through millions of webpages to find what you have requested. The first search engine, Archie, was developed by students at McGill University in Canada in 1989. In 1995, American computer students Sergey Brin and Larry Page began work on their Backrub search engine, which they renamed Google two years later. Google now handles billions of searches every day.

DIGITAL CAMERAS

Snap happy before digital cameras? You'd be clutching your bulky film camera and counting the cost per snap. These cameras gathered light and focused it onto a strip of film coated with light-sensitive chemicals. A roll of film held 12, 24, or 36 pictures and had to be chemically processed and printed at a photo lab before you got to see your snaps—a painful wait of days or weeks. You could develop black-and-white film in your own darkroom, if you had one, but it was time-consuming to bathe the film in chemicals before printing each photo by hand.

PERFECT PIXELS

A CCD is divided up into a grid of tiny squares called pixels. Each pixel measures the color and brightness of light that reaches it and turns these measurements into numbers. These numbers are then processed inside the camera and stored as an image file that can be viewed on a computer. The first CCD camera could record just 10,000 pixels. A modern camera's 20 million or more pixels allow much more detailed photos to be taken.

INVENTION: DIGITAL CAMERA

In 1975, Eastman Kodak engineer Steve Sassoon demonstrated the first portable digital camera. Instead of film, it used a silicon chip called a charged couple device (CCD). The camera weighed almost 8.8 pounds (4 kg)—20 times the weight of a small camera today. It took 23 seconds to record a small black-and-white photograph onto a cassette built into the camera.

GOING DIGITAL

Digital cameras became popular in the late 1990s. Images could be viewed instantly on camera screens and unwanted images deleted. As memory cards increased in capacity, a digital camera user could take thousands of photos. Today, an estimated 3.7 billion digital photos are taken every day.

PHONE CAMS

Mobile phones didn't get digital cameras until the 21st century —the first was the Sharp J-SH04 in 2000. It could only hold 20 photos, which then had to be downloaded onto a computer. Modern smartphone cameras can take thousands of quality photos or videos. Many news stories and events are now documented by phone cameras, and tiny digital cameras can be built into all sorts of devices, from watches to drones.

PERSONAL COMPUTERS

There were no digital computers in your home or office in the 1930s and 1940s. Almost all information was stored on paper—unbelievably large mounds of it! Documents all had to be handwritten or typed up using a typewriter, then filed and stored in giant records offices. Finding a fact, particular letter, or report could take you a LONG time!

EARLY COMPUTERS

The first computers, such as ENIAC in the USA and the Z series in Germany, were only used by the military and scientists. They filled whole rooms and relied on hundreds or thousands of large components, called valves, to act as switches when the computer made calculations. Programming these machines could take days and sometimes involved rewiring the computer by hand.

INVENTOR: GRACE HOPPER (1906–1992)

Computers were slow to program until the invention of compilers (a program that turns instructions that people can understand into commands a computer can act on). Programming pioneer Grace Hopper led the team that created the first compiler, the A-0, in 1952. Hopper also created the first computer language for business computers called FLOW-MATIC between 1955 and 1959.

SHRINKING TECH

The valves in computers were large, used lots of power, and sometimes broke down. They were replaced by much smaller and more reliable devices called transistors, invented in 1947 by a team at Bell Labs in the USA. Transistors got smaller and smaller until they could be etched onto a wafer of material smaller than your fingernail—a silicon chip. In 1971, the first microprocessor— a complete computing system on a single silicon chip—was developed by Ted Hoff and others at Intel.

COMPUTERS FOR ALL

Transistors and microprocessors transformed computers, making them smaller, cheaper, and more powerful. Information on paper was digitized—turned into files that could be stored, searched for, and used quickly on computers. Home computers like the Apple II, ZX Spectrum, and Commodore 64 appeared in the 1970s and 80s. They stored programs and information on cassette tapes and could take many minutes to load. Today, computers hold dozens of programs and thousands of files, all of which can be accessed in fractions of a second.

SEARCH AND RESCUE

Lost? Trapped? Fighting for survival? When disaster struck in times gone by you had to hope help was close at hand. After all, there were no mobile phones to send messages and no satellite navigation for you to be easily found by rescuers. Search parties might struggle to reach you, clambering over tough terrain or sailing along rocky coastlines.

HELPFUL HELICOPTERS

Regular aircraft must travel fast through the air for their wings to generate enough lift for them to fly. Helicopters can move far more slowly, even able to fly straight up or down and hover in midair. This makes them perfect for getting to hard-to-reach places, lowering supplies and medical staff, or winching people out of danger.

INVENTOR: IGOR SIKORSKY (1889–1972)

Born in Kiev, Ukraine, Sikorsky built his first model helicopter when he was just 12. In 1913, he constructed the world's first four-engined aircraft, the Russky Vityaz. Moving to the USA, Sikorsky built the VS-300 in 1939. This was the first practical helicopter powered by a single set of rotor blades. As with all his aircraft designs, Sikorsky insisted he made the first test flight before anyone else flew them. In 1945, a Sikorsky R-5 performed the first peacetime rescue by helicopter, when it winched five men to safety before their barge sank.

HOW IT WORKS

An engine spins a helicopter's rotor blades around. The blades are shaped like long, thin versions of an aircraft's wings. As the blades slice through the air, they generate a force called lift, raising the helicopter up into the air. By tilting the blades, air is pushed backward, moving the helicopter forward.

INVENTION: INFLATABLE LIFE JACKETS

Early life jackets were made of solid cork or stuffed full of kapok or foam, until Peter Markus's invention in 1928. His life jacket was easy to wear and featured small cylinders of carbon dioxide. When tabs were pulled, the jacket filled up with gas, making it float.

Main rotor unit can be tilted to steer helicopter forward, backward, or side to side

Spinning rotor blades generate lift

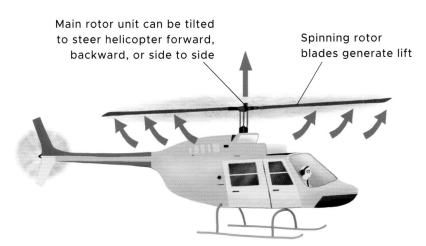

TELEVISION

Home time didn't mean television time in the early 1930s. There was no TV although your family might have a large valve radio which you'd all crowd around to listen to one of the few radio programs broadcast at the time. You'd learn news and information from newspapers and books, or by watching newsreels of world events at the cinema. Your free time, after chores and homework, would be spent playing games indoors or out, using mostly wooden or metal toys.

INVENTION: TELEVISION

Scottish engineer John Logie Baird was the first to broadcast moving pictures using his mechanical TV set in 1925. Baird's system displayed just 30 lines of detail in its pictures (today's HD TV has 1,080). It was overtaken by electronic television in the 1930s, which used bulky glass screens called cathode ray tubes.

EARLY VIEWING

Televisions were once giant boxes with small screens, and could cost a third of a yearly wage. They took minutes to warm up before displaying fuzzy black-and-white pictures of the few programs available to watch each day. Today's flat-screen TVs are much cheaper and larger, showing hundreds of TV channels around the clock.

BIG IMPACT

TV not only entertained, it educated and informed people and altered how many saw the world. For the first time, moving images from all over the planet—from nature documentaries to live sports and the latest world news—could be beamed into people's homes. TV viewing became the most common leisure activity at home.

An average person in the US today watches around 35.5 hours of TV a week—more than 12.6 years by the time you're 60 years old!

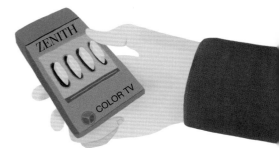

INVENTION: REMOTE CONTROL

People had to change channels or adjust the volume on the TV set, until the invention of the remote control in the 1950s. The first, called "Lazy Bones," was invented in 1950 and connected to a TV using a cable. The Flash-Matic, invented by Eugene Polley five years later, was cordless.

EMERGENCY TREATMENT

If you were a soldier at the start of World War I (1914–18), watch out! A terrifying 9.7 million military men and women died during the conflict, an average of 6,200 a day. As well as bullets and bombs, some artillery shells contained gases that caused serious injury or even death. Injuries that can be treated easily today, such as a broken leg or loss of blood, could kill at the time. Whatever your injury, your chances of survival depended on medical treatment and steering clear of infection—hard to do in the mud and squalor of the trenches and battlefield.

INVENTION: THE THOMAS SPLINT

In the first two years of the war, over 80 percent of soldiers who suffered a broken femur (upper leg bone) died from the injury, usually due to infection. Welsh surgeon Hugh Owen Thomas invented a special splint made from an iron frame covered in canvas. It kept a broken leg still and gave the best chance of the bone healing without infection. By the end of the war, the Thomas splint reduced soldiers' deaths from a broken femur to less than 10 percent.

BLOOD BANKS

Loss of blood led to many deaths in World War I as there were no large stores of blood for transfusions. In late 1917, US Army officer Oswald Robertson established small "blood depots," containing blood preserved in ice. In 1940, African-American surgeon Charles R. Drew discovered that plasma (the liquid part of blood) can be stored for far longer periods than whole blood. Drew helped create some of the first major blood banks in the USA.

MOBILE X-RAY UNITS

X-rays today are a valuable and common way for doctors to look inside the body, but they weren't available at many World War I battlefields. French scientist Marie Curie campaigned for a small fleet of motor vehicles, nicknamed Petites Curies. They were fitted with mobile X-ray scanners to help doctors locate bullets, shrapnel, and broken bones.

DISCOVERY: ANTIBIOTICS

In 1928, Scottish scientist Alexander Fleming discovered a mold that was destroying harmful bacteria in one of his experiments. The first-known antibiotic, Fleming named it penicillin. In the late 1930s and early 1940s, a team led by Howard Florey and Ernst Chain produced penicillin in large amounts, saving thousands of lives in World War II.

KITCHEN APPLIANCES

If you were hungry at home a hundred years ago, a snack from the fridge or an ice cream from the freezer wasn't on the menu. Homes didn't have these machines nor did they have microwave ovens or dishwashers. Fresh food needs to be kept cool to stop it from spoiling, so without fridges and freezers, you would shop for fresh food regularly and store it in snow outside or in a cool kitchen cupboard known as a larder. Some people kept food in an icebox, relying on large blocks of ice to keep it cool.

INVENTION: REFRIGERATOR

In 1748, Scottish scientist William Cullen discovered that when liquids evaporate (turn into gas or vapor), they absorb heat. This principle was used by a number of engineers to build the first cooling machines in the late 19th century. Fred W. Wolf invented one of the first electric home refrigerators in 1913, but fridges at home didn't become common until the late 1920s.

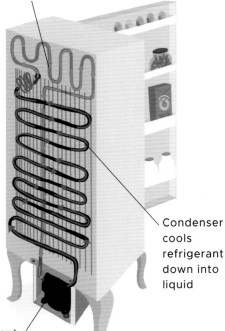

Cold refrigerant cools fridge interior by evaporation

Condenser cools refrigerant down into liquid

Compressor squeezes refrigerant

HOW FRIDGES WORK

A pump inside a fridge circulates a substance called a refrigerant around long, looping pipes. As the refrigerant turns from a liquid to a gas, it absorbs heat and keeps the inside of the fridge cool. The refrigerant is then squeezed by a pump called a compressor and turns back into a liquid in the condenser. A freezer works in the same way, but at lower temperatures.

INVENTOR: CLARENCE BIRDSEYE (1886–1956)

While working in Canada, American Clarence Birdseye watched Inuits freeze fish under thick ice really quickly. As the food was frozen suddenly, it kept its taste and texture. Birdseye returned to the USA and in the 1920s he used machines to flash-freeze food, which was then packed inside waxed cardboard cartons. Birdseye's innovations allowed people with a home freezer to enjoy seasonal vegetables, fish, and other foods all year round.

INVENTION: DISHWASHER

Wealthy American Josephine Cochran got annoyed at her servants chipping her crockery when washing up. She decided to do something about it and invented the first motorized dishwasher in 1886. It featured a copper boiler to spray hot water onto plates and cups that rotated on a slow-spinning wheel. Dishwashers became common in restaurants, but home dishwashers were rare until the 1950s. Today, over three-quarters of US homes have one.

LIFE BEFORE...
VACUUM CLEANERS

Expect to cough and splutter in your dusty home in the time before vacuum cleaners. If you were wealthy, your servants swept your rugs and carpets daily, but this just moved the dust around! Every now and then, you might take your carpets and rugs outside for a good beating, creating clouds of dust and dirt. Sometimes, you might have your carpets scrubbed in place, leaving them damp and smelly for days at a time. Pew!

INVENTION: VACUUM CLEANER

In the 1890s, cleaning machines pumped out air, hoping to blow dust off carpets and other items. British engineer Hubert Cecil Booth reversed the pump to suck rather than blow, carrying the dust down a pipe into a waste container. Booth's 1901 vacuum cleaner was far too large to enter a home. Instead, it was pulled by a horse and its long pipes were carried inside.

H CECIL BOOTH'S VACUUM

INVENTOR: JAMES SPANGLER (1848–1915)

James Spangler was an American caretaker who suffered from asthma, not helped by breathing in dust as he swept. In 1907, he built a handheld vacuum cleaner using a pillowcase as a dust bag, an electric fan, a tin box, and a motor from a sewing machine. Spangler's "Suction Sweeper" impressed his cousin Susan so much that her husband, William Hoover, bought all the rights to the machine. Millions of "Hoovers" were sold as vacuum cleaners and became common home cleaning machines.

INVENTOR: JAMES DYSON (b. 1947)

Some vacuum cleaners with dustbags lose their suction power as the bag gets full of dust. James Dyson experimented with an astonishing 5,127 different versions of his bagless vacuum cleaner before it finally went on sale in 1983. Dyson's vacuum cleaner featured a powerful motor, which sucks in dirt and then spins it around quickly. The dirt is flung out of the spinning air and falls to the bottom of the cleaner, where it is easily emptied.

Smaller cyclones clean air of finer particles

Spinning cyclone of air throws dirt outward

Air and dirt enter cleaner via brush bar

DUST-BUSTING DROIDS

The first robot vacuum cleaner, the Trilobite, was invented by Swedish company Electrolux in 1996. A rival model, the Roomba, launched in 2002 and is now the most common robot in the world with over 14 million machines sold. Each robot cleaner navigates itself around a room, avoiding stairs and obstacles such as furniture and keeping track of where it has already cleaned.

AIRCRAFT AND AIR TRAVEL

Can you imagine taking two months to travel from one country to another? That's how long a typical trip by ship once took between the UK and Australia. Long distance travel before planes really took its time, even in the mid-19th century when sailing ships were replaced by steam-powered ocean liners. Crossing the Atlantic between North America and Europe on a steam liner could take you 20 days at a speed of only 6–19 miles (10–30 km) per hour.

INVENTION: HEAVIER-THAN-AIR AIRCRAFT

Orville and Wilbur Wright owned a cycle repair shop in Ohio, USA. They became fascinated by flight and even built their own wind tunnel to study how flying worked. In December 1903, their Flyer 1 aircraft made the first powered sustained flight by a heavier-than-air plane. The flight lasted just 12 seconds and covered only 118 feet (36 m). The aircraft was powered by a small gasoline engine, which turned two propellers to push the plane forward.

PASSENGER PLANES

Early planes carried just one or two passengers, but in the 1920s larger aircraft were constructed that could carry 10–40 passengers over land or water. Jet engines allowed bigger and faster airliners to be built from the 1950s onward. The first jet airliner, the DH Comet, entered service in 1952 and six years later began nonstop flights across the Atlantic from New York to London. The journey sometimes took as little as 6.5 hours—a fraction of the time it took to cross by ship.

INVENTION: JET ENGINE

British engineer Frank Whittle and German scientist Hans von Ohain both invented jet engines in the 1930s. They produced more power than internal combustion engines. Air is drawn in through the front of the engine and mixed with fuel inside the combustion chamber. It is then set alight. As the mixture burns, large amounts of gases are produced and expand backward out of the engine, thrusting the aircraft forward.

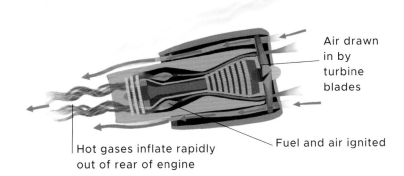

Air drawn in by turbine blades

Fuel and air ignited

Hot gases inflate rapidly out of rear of engine

FLYING FREIGHT

As planes increased their size and the distances they could fly, they became useful cargo carriers. Some 62 million tons of freight was carried by aircraft in 2017. Letters and parcels are delivered far faster than by land or sea, and fresh foods can now be flown in from the other side of the world without spoiling.

ANTISEPTICS AND ANESTHETICS

Imagine being wide awake as surgeons began cutting into your body or sawing off an arm or leg. The pain and shock alone could kill, which was why surgery before anesthetics and effective painkillers was only performed as a last resort. If you did manage to survive the shock of surgery, there was still a high chance of infection getting you afterward. Operations were often carried out in filthy conditions with unclean equipment.

DISCOVERY: NEW PAIN RELIEVERS

A number of substances were found to have a numbing effect on pain, including nitrous oxide gas, first discovered by English chemist Joseph Priestley in 1772. Chloroform was discovered in 1831 and first used as an anesthetic by Scottish doctor James Young Simpson in 1847. He used it to provide pain relief for women during childbirth, including Queen Victoria.

DISCOVERY: SLEEPING THROUGH SURGERY

A general anesthetic puts a patient into a controlled sleep so they cannot feel the pain of surgery. American dentist William T. Morton pioneered the use of ether as a general anesthetic in 1846 when he and two surgeons performed several operations as a demonstration. The use of anesthetics started spreading across the world, enabling complicated surgery to be performed successfully.

DISCOVERY: GERM THEORY

In the 1860s, French doctor Louis Pasteur suggested that germs—such as bacteria and viruses—could cause infections and diseases. At the time, most people thought that spirits or bad air were the cause. Germ theory was still not totally accepted as scientific fact until German scientist Robert Koch proved that diseases such as anthrax (in 1876) and tuberculosis (in 1882) were caused by bacteria. Surgeons began scrubbing hands and instruments before operations to help prevent infections.

INVENTION: DONKEY ENGINE

Inspired by Louis Pasteur's germ theory, British surgeon Joseph Lister started to clean the wounds of patients and soak bandages with carbolic acid—a substance that slowed down the growth of germs. He found infections occurred less often as a result. Lister built a pump he called a "donkey engine" to spray a mist of carbolic acid throughout the operating room before and during surgery.

LIFE BEFORE...
ASSEMBLY LINES

In the 19th century, building machines and other complex objects could be slow work. If you were a skilled craftsman you might make an entire product from start to finish on your own, by hand. Each of the finished items might be slightly different, making repairing or replacing parts difficult. A larger object, such as a train engine, might be worked on by many skilled people over months, making it expensive.

INTERCHANGEABLE PARTS
French gun maker Honoré Blanc pioneered the idea of making standardized parts for musket guns in the 1780s. Each part could be made in advance and replacement parts would fit and work perfectly. Blanc's idea caught on in the 19th century for a range of products, including typewriters, early bicycles, and sewing machines.

ASSEMBLY LINE
To meet demand for his motor car in 1901, Ransom Olds divided his workers up according to the groups of tasks they performed and kept them standing in one place. The frame of the car was moved in front of one group of workers who performed all their jobs before it was dragged off to the next group. This was the first car assembly line and increased production from 425 cars to 2,500 cars the following year.

INVENTION: MOVING ASSEMBLY LINE

American car maker Henry Ford took Olds' idea further. Ford broke down the assembly of one of his Model T cars into 84 steps and trained workers to perform just one step each. He used conveyor belts to automatically move the partly built cars along the assembly line where workers stood and performed their task over and over again. His first moving assembly line opened in Michigan in 1913. It slashed the time it took to build the body of a Model T car from 12 hours to just 93 minutes.

A robot arm welds metal parts together

RISE OF THE ROBOTS

Some assembly line jobs, such as those involving hot metals, chemicals, welding, or spraying paint, remained unpleasant for people until robots arrived. The first industrial robot, Unimate, was invented by Americans George Devol and Joseph Engelberger. In 1961, it worked in a General Motors car factory where it handled pieces of red-hot metal. Tens of thousands of robots have since entered factories, performing spray-painting, welding, and assembly tasks with perfect precision.

CARS

Before cars, many cities had a big poop problem. Buses, wagons, and carts were all pulled by horses —lots of them! New York City in 1880 contained 150,000 horses producing 3.3 million pounds (1.5 million kg) of manure on the streets every day! You would rely on horses or your own two legs, as most of your traveling would be done on foot. Some lucky people could take a train but only if there was a railway line nearby.

INVENTION: INTERNAL COMBUSTION ENGINE

Around 1860, Belgian engineer Jean Joseph Étienne Lenoir invented an engine that burned fuel inside a metal cylinder—one of the first internal combustion engines. German self-taught engineer Nikolaus Otto improved the design in 1876 to create the first practical internal combustion engine. It could be made small and light enough to power moving vehicles.

INVENTION: MOTOR CAR

In 1885, German engineer Carl Benz built the first car powered by a small internal combustion engine. His three-wheeled Motorwagen had a top speed of 10 miles (16 km) per hour and no steering wheel —the driver turned a lever to point the car's front wheel left or right. In 1894, Benz's next car, the Velo, had four wheels and was the first car to be made in large numbers, with 1,200 built. Today there are more than 1.2 billion motor vehicles on the world's roads.

TEST DRIVE DRAMA

In 1888, Benz's wife, Bertha, took their two sons in a Motorwagen on a 117-mile (189-km) drive from Mannheim to Pforzheim—the world's first long distance car journey. On the way back, she asked a shoe repairer to cover the car's worn brakes with hardwearing leather—inventing the first car brake lining. An American woman called Mary Anderson invented the first wipers to remove water and dirt from windshields 15 years later.

WORKING ENGINES

Air and fuel (usually gasoline) enter an engine's cylinders through an opening called a valve. The pistons move up inside the cylinders, squeezing the mixture, which makes it hotter. Spark plugs at the top of the cylinders produce sparks, which set the mixture alight. As the mixture burns, it produces hot, expanding gases, pushing the pistons back down the cylinders. A crank converts this up-and-down movement of the pistons into a turning movement, which powers the wheels.

Air and fuel burn, then hot gases push piston down

Piston moves up and down in its cylinder

Crankshaft creates turning power

THE TELEGRAPH AND TELEPHONES

A galloping horse may seem fast, but at 20–25 miles (30–40 km) per hour, it's no match for an email, text, or social media post that travels thousands of miles per second. Yet, for many centuries, a speeding horse was the fastest way for you to deliver a letter or message, taking 10 days or more from one side of the USA to the other. You could send simple messages by smoke signals, using fires on the tops of hills called beacons or, from the 1790s, by Frenchman Claude Chappe's system of semaphore towers, where wooden arms or people with flags signaled a message, letter by letter.

INVENTION: ELECTRICAL TELEGRAPH

In the 1830s, Samuel Morse in the USA and William Cooke and Charles Wheatstone in the UK both built telegraph systems that could send messages as pulses of electricity. These signals traveled along electrical wires at speeds far faster than a physical message could be transported.

LOTS OF LINES

The telegraph system sped up the movement of news and information hugely. By 1860, there were over 50,000 miles (80,000 km) of telegraph lines in the USA alone. Six years later, a giant telegraph cable was successfully laid along the floor of the Atlantic Ocean. Messages that had taken weeks to travel on ships between Europe and North America could now be sent and received in minutes.

INVENTOR: SAMUEL MORSE (1791–1872)

As well as building one of the first telegraph systems, Samuel Morse invented a system of short pulses (dots) and longer pulses (dashes) of electricity to represent the letters of the alphabet. Morse code was used by skilled operators to tap telegraph messages quickly —up to 50 words a minute.

INVENTION: TELEPHONE

While working on improvements to the telegraph in 1876, Alexander Graham Bell invented the first practical working telephone. A metal cone collected sound waves and turned the vibrations into electrical signals that could be sent along wires. When the signals reached the receiving telephone, they were converted back into sound through a loudspeaker. Within five years, there were over 45,000 telephones in the USA, and by 1900 there were millions of phones all over the world. Switchboards allowed different phone lines to connect to each other by an operator plugging in wires. Two sisters, Emma and Stella Nutt, became the first female switch operators in 1878.

STEAM TRAINS

No holidays, city breaks, or vacations for you if you lived in the 1800s. Most people rarely traveled far because transport was so, so slow. Horse drawn carts and carriages moved sluggishly and river barges, which could carry larger amounts of goods, were even slower. They rarely reached speeds much above a brisk walking pace. As a result, you would eat fresh foods close to where they were produced, as they would perish in the days it took to complete a long journey.

INVENTION: STEAM LOCOMOTIVE

Mine engineers harnessed the power of steam engines to power the wheels of the first steam locomotives. Richard Trevithick built the first full-sized, practical steam locomotive, which ran at Penydarren ironworks in Wales, in 1804. The steam trains that followed hauled wagons of coal or rock at mines and ironworks.

Smoke escapes through chimney

Steam from boiler turns large flywheel that drives wheels around

Wheels turn and move along iron track

ROCKETING AWAY

Trials were held in England in 1829 to find the quickest and most reliable steam locomotive. Robert Stephenson's *Rocket* won hands-down. The following year, the first public railway between cities—Liverpool and Manchester—was opened using Stephenson's trains, with a top speed of 30 miles (48 km) per hour. Today's high speed trains, like France's TGV or Japan's Shinkansen, race along at up to 200 miles (320 km) per hour.

INVENTOR: GRANVILLE T. WOODS

A self-taught African-American engineer, Woods invented a number of innovations that made railway journeys quicker and safer, including a braking system that used compressed air. In 1887, his multiplex telegraph system allowed messages to be sent between moving trains and stations. This helped measure the distances between trains to avoid crashes.

ON TRACK

Trains proved a big hit, allowing goods and people to be carried quickly from place to place. Railway building boomed in the UK and throughout the world. By 1900, there was over 187,500 miles (300,000 km) of track in the US alone—enough to circle the entire Earth 7.5 times.

ROCKET

LIFE BEFORE...
ELECTRIC LIGHT

Life could be gloomy if you lived before electric lights. Most work was carried out between dawn and dusk, as after sunset everywhere descended into darkness. With little street lighting, sneaky thieves were able to escape easily into the shadows. Inside your dimly lit home, you might try to read, clean, or sew clothes using just candlelight, a small gas lantern, or oil lamp. The risk of fire was great.

INVENTION: ARC LAMP

In 1807, English scientist Humphry Davy attached two rods of charcoal to an early electric battery. His arc lamp produced a bright light between the two rods for a short time. Davy's experiment showed that some materials produced light when electricity flowed through them. Arc lamps were improved to become the first electric lights used in large factories and as street lighting in some cities.

LIGHT BULB MOMENTS

Most people continued to live in gloom until the invention of the incandescent light bulb—glass containers holding a thin filament that glowed when heated to very high temperatures by electricity. In 1880, after 20 years of work, Joseph Swan's house in England became the first to be lit by electric light bulbs. Swan's initial bulbs lasted for a handful of hours. Thomas Edison performed over 4,000 experiments on light bulbs in the late 1870s and early 1880s, eventually finding that filaments made of bamboo lasted up to 1,200 hours.

LIGHT UP YOUR LIFE

Incandescent light bulbs offered easy, safe, bright lighting at the flick of a switch. A 60-watt light bulb produced about as much light as 100 candles, enabling people to work and do other things in winter and the dark of night. As electricity became more widely available, more homes and buildings used electric lighting.

LIGHT AND COLOR

Lights all gave off white or slightly yellow light until neon lights were invented by French scientist Georges Claude. The first went on public display in 1910. These glass tubes contain gas which gives off colored light when electricity passes through. When filled with neon gas, the lights emit a red glow, while mercury gas makes the light shine blue. Neon lights were used to create colorful advertising signs.

39

FIRE ENGINES

"Fire!" You'd hear that cry a lot if you lived in the past. Buildings in towns were mostly made of wood with straw roofs and people used open fires for cooking and candles for light. When a fire raged, it could sweep through an entire neighborhood quickly. In the 1650s, fires destroyed a third of Glasgow, two thirds of the Japanese city of Edo (modern day Tokyo), and 4,664 houses in Aachen, Germany. If you spotted a fire breaking out, you had little more than buckets of water and next-to-no protective clothing.

PUMPING WATER

Fires were often fought using small hand water pumps, known as squirts. They worked a little like a bicycle pump, drawing in about half a gallon (2 liters) of water and then pumping it out at the fire. In the 1720s, English inventor Richard Newsham built a fire-fighting pump on wheels with a tank that held 170 gallons (640 liters) of water. With 4–12 people operating the pump, by pulling levers up and down, it could spray over 80 gallons (300 liters) of water a minute.

INVENTION: STEAM-POWERED FIRE ENGINES

One of the very first steam-powered fire engines was invented by English engineer John Braithwaite in 1829. It could squirt water up to a height of 88 feet (27 m)—ideal for tackling blazes in tall buildings. Fire engines were pulled slowly by horses, but by the 1900s, fire engines could race to the scene, powered by internal combustion engines.

INVENTION: FOAM VS FIRES

Some types of blazes, such as oil fires, are not easily put out with water. In 1902, Russian schoolteacher Aleksandr Loran invented a foam that covered the fuel, stopping oxygen from reaching the fire, which put it out. Foam or water is today sprayed from fire extinguishers—small cylinders that use compressed air. The first portable fire extinguisher was a copper cylinder by English inventor George Manby in 1817.

FIRE HYDRANTS

To tackle big fires you need a large supply of water. In the past, firefighters were often supplied with water by "bucket brigades" made up of chains of people passing buckets of water from a well or pond. Fire hydrants started to be built in the 19th century. These fittings tapped into a town's mains water pipes and allowed firefighters to attach a hose for a constant supply of water.

THE TEXTILES INDUSTRY

Fashion fads, changing clothes, and worrying over what to wear each day were not problems in the past for the majority. Unless you were very wealthy, you'd have few clothes, since cloth was expensive. It was made slowly by hand, often by entire families in the countryside. Using a simple spinning wheel, you might spin wool or cotton into long strands of thread. This might be dyed before a weaver wove the strands of yarn together using a handloom. A few feet of cloth might take hours to make.

INVENTION: POWER LOOM

In 1785, English clergyman Edmund Cartwright invented a mechanical loom. Powered by waterwheels and, later, steam engines, these machines could weave cloth far faster than a handloom. Many engineers made improvements to Cartwright's invention and by 1850, there were over 250,000 power looms weaving cloth in England alone.

INVENTOR: RICHARD ARKWRIGHT (1732–1792)

In the 1760s, British wigmaker Richard Arkwright developed the water frame, using waterwheels to power machines that spun vast amounts of thread. In 1771, Arkwright and his business partners set up a spinning and weaving factory in Cromford. He went on to install steam engines to power his machines. By 1800, there were 900 giant mills in Britain, using water frames and power looms to produce feet of metres of cloth.

INVENTION: COTTON GIN

As the textiles industry boomed, demand for raw materials, especially cotton, soared. Cotton took time to clean and remove seeds for its fibers—a day for one worker to clean less than 2.2 pounds (1 kg) of cotton. In 1793, Eli Whitney and Catherine Greene developed the cotton gin in the USA. This machine used a series of steel discs with hooks to drag the cotton fibers through slots, leaving the seeds behind. As much as 50 times more cotton could be cleaned each day.

FACTORY IMPACT

All these innovations meant that far more cloth could be produced than before. Trade and ports boomed in cotton-growing nations, such as India and the USA, and in cloth-making centers, such as Britain and France. Thousands of people moved from the countryside to work in ports and mill towns as cloth-making became a massive industry.

LIFE BEFORE...
TOILETS AND SANITATION

Life in many cities of the past was far less hygienic and far more stinky than today. With no sewage pipes to carry waste away from homes, you'd go to the toilet in a chamber pot – a small bowl with a handle. You would empty this into a river, an open hole in the ground called a cesspit, or throw it out of an upstairs window into the street...watch out below! Cesspits full of poop had to be emptied and their smelly contents taken to farms as fertilizer. Nearby ponds and rivers were often polluted by waste and became breeding grounds for disease.

FLUSHED WITH SUCCESS

Some ancient civilizations built toilets and sewage systems over 4,000 years ago. Cities in the Indus Valley built stone and mud brick toilets. Water ran along channels or pipes made of terracotta below the toilets to carry the poop and pee away from houses and out of the city. The ancient Romans had communal toilets where everyone sat in a row. Instead of toilet paper, people wiped themselves with a sponge on the end of a stick!

INVENTOR: SIR JOHN HARINGTON

In the 1590s, Sir John Harington invented a flushing toilet, named Ajax. He showed it to his godmother who just happened to be Queen Elizabeth I! When a lever was pulled, a leather flap in a cistern (water tank) opened and water flooded out, forcing the waste out of the toilet and down a pipe.

44

INVENTION: GOING AROUND THE BEND

Flushing toilets didn't catch on until they were improved 200 years later. In 1775, Scottish watchmaker Alexander Cumming invented a flushing toilet that had a pipe bent in the shape of an "S" under the toilet bowl. This trapped water below the bowl, stopping smelly gases rising from the sewage pipes into the bathroom.

DISCOVERY: CLEAN THINKING

Scientists in the 19th century began to understand more about how unclean water helped cause disease. In 1855, English scientist John Snow discovered that cholera was spread by dirty water. Many cities built networks of sewage pipes to carry waste away and keep it separate from clean water. As a result, diseases like typhoid, cholera, and dysentery struck less often and people started to live healthier and longer lives.

THE PRINTING PRESS

Listen up! In the days before speedy printing, you'd receive news or instructions mostly by word of mouth. Information might be posted in a crowded square or read aloud by a town crier. Only a small number of books were produced, mostly handwritten by scribes or monks. They were expensive—costing more than a worker's yearly wage! As a result, news, scientific discoveries, and the latest knowledge tended to spread slowly.

INVENTION: MOVABLE TYPE

Printing that used a carved wooden block was first invented in China over 1,000 years ago. By 1200, Koreans were printing using pieces of metal showing different characters. This movable metal type could be arranged in a frame to spell out words and then covered in ink before it was pressed down onto paper to print a page. The type could then be arranged to print different pages so that copies of books could be made far faster than writing out each word by hand.

PRINTING HITS EUROPE

German blacksmith and printer Johannes Gutenberg introduced movable type printing to Europe around 1450. He built a printing press based on presses used in farming to squeeze grapes and olives. He also made an oil-based ink that stuck well to the paper. Although Gutenberg did not strike it rich with his invention, printing spread rapidly through Europe.

STEAMING IN

In 1812, Germans Andreas Bauer and Friedrich Koenig invented a high-speed, steam-powered printing press. Five times faster than previous presses, it was first used to print *The Times* newspaper in 1814. Books and newspapers began to be produced more cheaply, with paperback books becoming popular from the 1860s onward.

INVENTION: BOOKS FOR THE BLIND

Blind French teenager Louis Braille developed his own ingenious system of writing in 1824. Braille used a grid of up to six raised dots to represent each letter or number. Embossed onto pages, visually impaired people could now enjoy reading by tracing the raised dots with their fingertips.

h e l l o

GUNPOWDER

Your army has a castle surrounded 1,000 years ago!
You might be in for a long wait as a siege could last
weeks or months if the walls were strong. Without
gunpowder, the deadliest weapons your army could
wield were siege engines—wooden machines like
catapults for flinging rocks or battering rams for
smashing down castle doors. You might be armed
with swords, spears, and bows and arrows, but
neither siege engines nor your own weapons were
a match for stout stone walls.

INVENTION: BLACK POWDER

Around 850 CE, Chinese scientists experimented with mixing
saltpeter with charcoal and sulfur. The resulting black powder,
a type of gunpowder, burned fiercely when lit and was first
used to create flaming arrows. When more saltpeter was
added, the powder became explosive. By 1000 CE, Chinese
soldiers were using bamboo tubes filled with gunpowder to
fire arrows or sharp pieces of metal at an enemy.

BLAST!

People found uses for
gunpowder in peacetime
as well. In 1627, Hungarian
engineer Caspar Weindel
packed gunpowder into holes
drilled into rock to blast it
away. This technique became
widely used to remove rock
when quarrying or mining.

INVENTION: CANNONS

By around 1350, some European armies were using cannons in battle. These large bronze or iron tubes used a charge of gunpowder to fire a heavy stone or metal ball with great force.

WALL BUSTER

When Turkish Ottoman forces attacked the city of Constantinople in 1453 they used giant bronze cannons, made by a Hungarian engineer called Orban. The cannons battered down the walls of the city, leading to victory. Suddenly, castles and cities surrounded by thick stone walls were no longer safe from attack.

THE COMPASS

Thousands of years ago, life as a sailor was risky. If you traveled on a wooden boat or ship it may seem sturdy, but without GPS, compass, radio, or accurate maps and charts, the crew might struggle to find the way. Most voyages would be kept short and during the daytime, sailing close to shore so that you could spot landmarks along the coast. Some sailors tried to follow flocks of birds or use the positions of the stars in the night sky to work out where they were heading. Many boats and ships got lost and some never reached their destination.

INVENTION: COMPASS

Earth is surrounded by a magnetic field. When a magnet moves freely, one of its ends, called its north pole, always points to north. Chinese scientists discovered this phenomenon over 2,200 years ago when they found a magnetized iron mineral called lodestone. Chinese builders used a lodestone compass, sometimes in a shape of a spoon, to align a house or temple so that it faced a direction associated with good fortune.

COMPASS AHOY!

Compasses didn't find their way onto ships for more than 1,000 years. The first compasses on Chinese trading ships and later Arabic and European vessels, were often iron needles rubbed against a piece of lodestone to turn them into a magnet. The needle was then placed on a piece of straw and floated in a bowl of water to point north.

INVENTION: MARINER'S ASTROLABE

Adopted by sailors in the 15th century, brass astrolabes measured the angle between a ship and the Sun or a night-time star. This helped work out latitude—how far north or south the ship was at sea. Today, ships use a range of electronic instruments as well as radio contact with ports to know their precise location at all times.

AGE OF DISCOVERY

Astrolabes and compasses helped spark a period of sea exploration by sailors from Asia and Europe. In 1498, Portugal's Vasco da Gama discovered a sea route from Europe around Africa to India and the rest of southern Asia. Spanish sailors traveled the Atlantic Ocean to discover islands in the Caribbean and in Central America. Further expeditions brought back exotic new foods to Europe for the first time, including potatoes, pineapples, and tomatoes.

LIFE BEFORE...
PAPER

In the days before paper, you would write and draw on all sorts of materials—from strips of wood and flattened palm leaves to clay tablets, pieces of broken pottery, and sheets of expensive silk. Ancient Roman schoolkids often wrote on wooden tablets covered with wax. They used a pointed stylus to carve letters into the wax. Instead of "books," ancient schools had scrolls, although these were rare. The scrolls were made of papyrus reeds, pounded and dried into long sheets.

INVENTION: PAPER

Paper was first made in China. The earliest-recorded paper-maker was a Chinese court official called Ts'ai Lun, around 104 CE. His paper proved much lighter in weight, cheaper, and easier to make than other materials. It was so good that Chinese emperors kept paper a secret for hundreds of years. It didn't spread to other parts of Asia until 600–800 CE and to Europe centuries later.

MAKING PAPER

Early paper was made by soaking plant fibers, such as tree bark and hemp, with shredded rags in water, and then mashing the fibers into a wet pulp. This was strained and pressed onto a frame and then hung up or laid out to dry in the sun. The end result was a sheet of interlocked fibers that formed a flexible, easy-to-write-on material.

MONEY, MONEY, MONEY

Ancient China used copper coins strung together on a rope as money. These could be heavy and cumbersome, so merchants and other wealthy people left their coins with someone they trusted and received a note promising they'd get their coins back. Around 960CE, the Chinese government, short of copper to make coins, started issuing similar notes printed on paper, called Jiaozi. These were the first paper bank notes.

SKIP TO THE LOO

Toilet paper was also invented in China. By 1391CE, China's Bureau of Imperial Supplies was producing 720,000 sheets for the emperor and his family. Everyone else used moss, rags, leaves, or their hands! The first roll of toilet paper didn't arrive until the 1880s, made by a US company. Today, every person in the US uses as much as 141 toilet rolls each year!

CONSTRUCTION MACHINES

You'd struggle to find your friends at an ancient Egyptian building site as thousands of people worked there. Without big construction machines like cranes and bulldozers, all the work had to be done by hand. This included cutting, smoothing, and dragging giant stone blocks into place to form temples and pyramids. The Great Pyramid at Giza contained a staggering 2.3 million limestone blocks, each weighing many tons. That's a lot of work! Workers' own homes were smaller, simpler, and often made from mud bricks left to dry in the sun.

INVENTION: CRANE

The ancient Greeks invented the first cranes around 2,600 years ago. They used wooden frames and a series of ropes to raise stone blocks faster and more easily. Ancient Roman engineers, wanting to lift even larger loads, developed polyspastos cranes. These giant wooden cranes were powered by people moving a treadmill and could lift up to 13,200 pounds (6,000 kg).

INVENTOR: ARCHIMEDES (c.287–212BCE)

Ancient Greek thinker and inventor Archimedes is thought to have devised the first block-and-tackle pulley system. It winds ropes around a series of pulley wheels to increase the distance the rope travels when pulled, meaning less force is needed to lift a load. Block and tackles fitted to cranes enabled them to lift heavier loads, using animals such as oxen to provide the power.

INVENTION: CONCRETE

Concrete is made from a mixture of small pieces of rock and stone bound together by cement. Many ancient civilizations discovered and used concrete. It was the ancient Romans, however, in 200 BCE, who found that adding a type of ash from volcanoes, called pozzolana, made concrete much stronger and more water resistant.

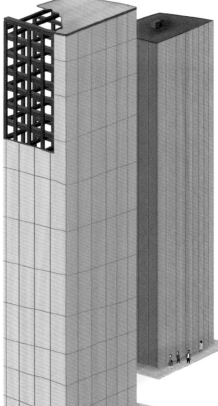

MODERN MATERIALS

In the 1850s, Henry Bessemer developed a process for making large amounts of strong steel cheaply. Steel became a common building material, both as a frame for tall buildings and as rods running through concrete panels to make concrete even stronger. Using reinforced concrete and steel, towering skyscrapers were constructed for the first time.

LIFE BEFORE...
THE WHEEL

Thousands of years ago, transporting things could be back-breaking work...literally. Heavy loads like firewood or harvested crops might be humped around on your back or dragged along the ground using ropes. Even with the help of strong animals, such as oxen, moving big things like stone blocks or tree trunks could be tough, slow, exhausting work. Therefore, many objects weren't moved very far at all.

A WHEEL WELCOME

The very first wheels, invented in Mesopotamia over 5,500 years ago, were used for making pottery. People spun wheels around by hand to shape clay into pots. Then someone had the idea to turn two potter's wheels on their side and let them spin around an axle. The result was a machine that could roll rather than slide across the ground, creating much less friction (a force which slows objects down).

WAGONS HO!

Wagons and carts fitted with pairs of wheels suddenly became popular in the Middle East and Europe from around 3150BCE. When pulled by animals such as oxen, wagons filled with large loads could be transported with ease.

CHARGE!

The first wheels were solid, heavy pieces of wood. Around 4,000 years ago, wheels with spokes were invented. This meant that far lighter wheels and faster vehicles could be built. Two-wheeled chariots pulled by galloping horses were first used in battle by the Hyksos and Hittites around 3,700 years ago.

INVENTION: TIRES

Wooden or metal wheels stayed unchanged for centuries. They worked well, but gave a bumpy ride. In 1845, Scottish engineer Robert W. Thomson invented a rubber tire filled with air. It didn't catch on until John Boyd Dunlop developed a version, 43 years later. These air-filled tires absorbed bumps and jolts when traveling over uneven ground, giving a more comfortable journey.

FARMING

Around 15,000 years ago there were no supermarkets, cafes, or even farms growing crops or rearing animals. You might snack on berries, hoping they weren't poisonous, or a big, tasty handful of insects. Ugh! You may also fish or hunt creatures of all sizes, right up to gigantic woolly mammoths, using just rocks or sharpened branches as spears. Life was always on the move as the seasons changed and you would follow animals as they moved to new places to graze.

FIRST FARMERS

More than 10,000 years ago, people began capturing young wild goats, pigs, and sheep. They tamed and raised them to provide meat and milk. People in the Middle East and elsewhere began planting seeds and growing crops, including wheat, chickpeas, and barley. As people began farming, their lifestyle changed and they could stay in the same place for most or all of the year.

INVENTION: SCRATCH PLOW

Around 7,500 years ago, people in Mesopotamia (modern-day Iraq) began using pieces of wood bound together to prepare their fields. This scratch plow, pulled by animals such as oxen, featured a piece of pointed wood that dug a long groove in the ground—perfect for planting seeds. The plow made it easier to farm larger areas of land and produce bigger crops to feed more people.

INVENTION: FLAIL

Ancient peoples learned how to crush cereal grains, such as wheat and barley, to make flour for bread. Separating the grains from the rest of the plant was slow, painstaking work, until the invention of the flail around 5,000 years ago. A flail consists of two sticks joined by a chain or leather strap used to beat a crop to knock the grains away from the rest of the plant. A modern combine harvester can thresh thousands of times more grain.

IRRIGATION

The earliest farmers relied on rain or nearby rivers flooding their banks to bring water to their crops. Around 8,000 years ago, Sumerians (from modern-day Iraq) began digging channels and ditches to carry water from rivers to their fields. Later, water was stored in ponds and reservoirs farther away for when water was in short supply. Irrigation enabled more and more land, especially in hot, dry regions, to grow crops.

INTO THE FUTURE

Look how far we've come! In quite a short time compared to the overall history of Earth, people have learned how to shape their surroundings, fashion incredible materials and machines, and live, work, travel, and play in a great variety of ways. Think about how different your life would be without each invention or discovery covered in this book!

However, the story of invention and innovation is far from over. Scientists, engineers, and ingenious inventors are working today on products and processes that might change your life tomorrow.

We cannot be certain what the future will bring but we can expect to see many advances in the years ahead. You might encounter exciting smart vehicles powered in eco-friendly ways, buildings made of amazing new materials, and advanced generations of robots and other smart devices in towns and cities. Whatever the future brings, it will build on all the great breakthroughs made in the past. Which could you not live without?

GLOSSARY

ANESTHETIC
substance used by doctors to stop you from feeling pain during an operation

BACTERIA
tiny single-celled living things that thrive in a wide range of different surroundings. Many bacteria are helpful and found inside the human body, while others can cause illness and disease.

BOILER
device or chamber in which water is heated to create hot water or steam

CAPACITY
in computing, the amount of data that a memory card or other storage device can hold

COMBUSTION
commonly known as burning, this is the chemical reaction involving a fuel, oxygen, and some form of heat or spark which results in lots of heat and light energy

CONTAMINATE
to make something no longer pure by adding a polluting or harmful substance

EMBOSS
to mold, press, or stamp a design on an object or surface so that it stands out

EVAPORATE
when a liquid turns into a gas or vapor

EXPERIMENT
to try out new ideas, techniques, or inventions, often using scientific methods

FRICTION
force or resistance that one surface or object encounters when moving over another. Friction tends to slow down moving objects.

GPS
short for Global Positioning System, this is a series of satellites orbiting Earth which provide pinpoint navigation on the planet's surface

INFECTION
invasion of the body by bacteria and other harmful germs that can cause disease

INTERNAL COMBUSTION ENGINE
type of engine that produces power when fuel and air or oxygen are burned inside a chamber. Gasoline engines used in many motor vehicles are internal combustion engines.

IRRIGATION
system of channels and reservoirs that supplies water to farm fields to help grow crops

LOCOMOTIVE
powered railway vehicle used to pull other railway carriages or wagons

NAVIGATE
to find your way

PISTON
rod that can move back and forth inside a tube called a cylinder

PROGRAMMING
in computing, producing a series of instructions that a computer or other digital device carries out

ROBOT
machine capable of performing a complex set of tasks with little or no human supervision

SATELLITE
human-made machines that orbit the Earth and perform a variety of jobs, including mapping the Earth's surface and relaying computer data and TV signals

STANDARDIZE
to make something to a particular standard so that it matches others

TONNE
metric tonne equal to 1,000 kilograms or 2,204.6 pounds

TRANSFUSION
process of adding an amount of new blood into a human or animal's body

TRANSISTOR
tiny electronic component that can act as a switch or amplifier. Millions of transistors can be squeezed onto a microchip.

WATERWHEEL
machine that produces power from flowing or falling water

WELDING
method of joining two pieces of metal using high temperatures to melt their surfaces together

TIMELINE

3150BCE
The first carts and wagons with wheels are built in parts of Europe and the Middle East.

400BCE
The ancient Greeks invent the first cranes. These enabled large loads to be lifted more easily than before.

200BCE
The Romans discover how to make a form of strong, hardwearing concrete using volcanic ash.

100–200BCE
The ancient Chinese invent the first compass, which uses lodestone to point north.

104CE
A Chinese official, Ts'ai Lun, describes how paper is made for the first time.

1807
Humphry Davy invents the first electric arc light.

1817
The first portable fire extinguisher is created by English inventor George Manby.

1824
The Braille writing and reading system for the visually impaired is developed by Frenchman Louis Braille.

1830
The first intercity railway that carries passengers and goods by steam train is opened between Manchester and Liverpool.

1837
Samuel Morse in the US and William Cooke and Charles Wheatstone in the UK produce the first practical versions of the telegraph system for sending and receiving messages.

1888
A practical pneumatic tire, made of rubber and filled with air, is developed by John Boyd Dunlop.

1901
The first motor-driven vacuum suction cleaner is unveiled by Hubert Cecil Booth in the UK.

1903
Orville and Wilbur Wright make the first sustained flight in a heavier-than-air craft.

1910
Neon lights, developed by French engineer Georges Claude, are used in public for the first time.

1913
The first moving assembly line for mass producing cars is introduced by Henry Ford in the US.

1961
The first industrial robot, the Unimate, begins work in a US car factory.

1964
The first Shinkansen high-speed bullet train begins service between Tokyo and Shin-Osaka in Japan.

1971
Ted Hoff at Intel invents the microprocessor —a complete computing system on a small chip.

1978
The first experimental Global Positioning System (GPS) satellite is launched from the US.

1983
The first cellular mobile phone, produced by US electronics company Motorola, goes on sale.

850ce
Gunpowder is developed in China, first used for fireworks and, later, weapons.

1450
Johannes Gutenberg develops the first movable type printing press in Europe.

1590s
Sir John Harington invents an early flushing toilet with a water tank in England.

1785
The power loom is invented by Edmund Cartwright in England, increasing the speed at which cloth can be woven.

1793
Eli Whitney and Catherine Greene invent the cotton gin, a machine that cleans cotton quicker than by hand, helping to speed up cotton production.

1856
The Bessemer process to produce strong, cheap steel is patented by English inventor Henry Bessemer.

1868
A 33-foot (10-m)-tall aerial ladder, for use with fire engines, is invented by New York volunteer firefighter Daniel D. Hayes.

1877
The first commercial telephone line is operational, using telephones patented by Alexander Graham Bell.

1885
Karl Benz builds the first motor car powered by an internal combustion engine.

1885
The first modern skyscraper building is completed in Chicago, USA, using steel and concrete in its construction.

1925
John Logie Baird broadcasts the first moving pictures using his mechanical television set.

1928
Penicillin is discovered by Alexander Fleming and becomes the world's first antibiotic.

1938
The first programmable computer, the Z1, is developed by Konrad Zuse in Germany.

1945
The first rescue performed by helicopter is made by a Sikorsky R-5, retrieving five men from a sinking barge.

1949
The world's first jet airliner, the de Havilland Comet, makes its first test flight.

1957
The first human-made satellite, Sputnik, is sent into space by the Soviet Union.

1984
Geneticist Alec Jeffreys invents DNA fingerprinting (DNA profiling), which is now used in criminal investigations.

1991
The world's first website goes online, produced by the inventor of the World Wide Web, Tim Berners-Lee.

1998
Stanford University students Sergey Brin and Larry Page launch their Google search engine for the World Wide Web.

2005
The world's largest airliner, the Airbus A380, makes its first passenger flight, taking off from France.

2008
Apple and Android both open app stores for users to download useful apps onto their smartphones or tablets.

INDEX